David

Rober

Marsha Kline Pruett

Dee Speese-Linehan

How to Prepare for and Respond to a Crisis

2nd Edition

ASSOCIATION FOR SUPERVISION AND CURRICULUM DEVELOPMENT • ALEXANDRIA, VIRGINIA • USA

Association for Supervision and Curriculum Development
1703 N. Beauregard St. • Alexandria, VA 22311-1714 USA
Telephone: 800-933-2723 or 703-578-9600 • Fax: 703-575-5400
Web site: http://www.ascd.org • E-mail: member@ascd.org

ASCD publications present a variety of viewpoints. The views expressed or implied in this book should not be interpreted as official positions of the Association.

All Web links in this book are correct as of the publication date below but may have become inactive or otherwise modified since that time. If you notice a deactivated or changed link, please e-mail books@ascd.org with the words "Link Update" in the subject line. In your message, please specify the Web link, the book title, and the page number on which the link appears.

ISBN: 0-87120-722-2   ASCD product no.: 103029   s9/02
ASCD member price: $15.95   nonmember price: $18.95

Library of Congress Cataloging-in-Publication Data
How to prepare for and respond to a crisis / David J. Schonfeld . . . [et al.].— 2nd ed.
    p. cm.
Includes bibliographical references (p.).
  ISBN 0-87120-722-2 (alk. paper)
  1. School crisis management—United States. 2. Crisis intervention (Mental health services)—United States. 3. Schools—United States—Safety measures. 4. School psychology—United States. I. Schonfeld, David J., 1959– II. Association for Supervision and Curriculum Development.
  LB2866.5 .H68 2002
  363.11'9371—dc21

                                                    2002009497

08 07 06 05 04 03 02   10 9 8 7 6 5 4 3 2 1

How to Prepare for
and Respond to a Crisis
2nd Edition

PREFACE

DEALING WITH THE EFFECTS OF A CRISIS ON SCHOOLCHILDREN AND STAFF
is not the primary mission of schools, nor is it the reason why
most educators or school administrators entered the profes-
sion. Not surprisingly, therefore, many schools do not plan for
or prepare to respond to a crisis that might affect their students and staff. As a result, at the time of a large-scale crisis,
such as the one precipitated by the attacks on the World Trade
Center in New York City and the Pentagon in Washington,
D.C., on Sept. 11, 2001, school staff are in turmoil. As members of the school and the broader community, they are likely
to be personally affected by the same crisis confronting their
students and may be more directly affected. Staff may be
unable to organize an effective crisis intervention response
and to maintain the long-range perspective that is needed. In
addition, staff may underestimate the full impact of the crisis
or feel overwhelmed by the extent, magnitude, and personal
nature of the problems. The bottom line is that it is hard to
plan a coordinated response at the time of a crisis.

The regional crisis committee established in 1991 has evolved into the School Crisis Prevention and Response Initiative of the National Center for Children Exposed to Violence (www.nccev.org)—a collaboration of the Yale Child Study Center and community mental health professionals, law enforcement representatives, and local and state educational agencies. Our mission is to empower school staff through prior planning and training, to help schools develop their capacity to meet the emotional and mental health needs of students and staff in times of crisis, and to provide technical assistance in resolving problems arising in specific crisis situations. In 10 years, we have provided training in more than half the school districts in Connecticut, as well as in school systems throughout the country, and have provided technical assistance during hundreds of school crisis events. Following the events of Sept. 11, 2001, the Board of Education of New York City created the Partnership for Recovery in the New York City Schools. The National Center for Children Exposed to Violence began working with the Partnership shortly afterward. The School Crisis Prevention and Response Initiative is now helping to coordinate school crisis response and training for the system, composed of 1,200 schools serving more than 1.1 million students.

The crisis response model that our group developed is a programmatic model. It provides structure at a time of crisis and ensures that key issues are considered, appropriate steps are taken, and necessary resources are in place. Such planning allows schools to take advantage of the staff's expertise in child development, experience in supporting children, and personal knowledge of the student population. We have found that adequately prepared school-based crisis teams can respond effectively to the majority of crisis events that affect school communities. In the absence of planning and preparation, however, schools often fail to realize this potential.

It is a sobering fact that children and schools have more need for school crisis response planning now than when the first edition of this book was prepared. Our experience has shown that not only is the topic timely, but 52the advice and best practices described within the book remain critical. We hope that you find the information helpful in planning how best to prepare your school community for the next crisis event.

ACKNOWLEDGMENTS

THE AUTHORS APPRECIATE THE ONGOING CONTRIBUTIONS OF SCOTT Newgass to the work of the School Crisis Prevention and Response Initiative. Scott Newgass is the program's Technical Assistance Coordinator.

1

PREPARING FOR A CRISIS

IN THE WINTER OF 1991, AS A GRIM NATION BRACED ITSELF FOR THE Persian Gulf War, the Yale Child Study Center convened a forum of university, public school, community, and government agency professionals to address the mental health needs of schoolchildren during the crisis. Fortunately, the international threat was soon resolved. Participants in the forum, however, quickly dismissed the notion of disbanding. They resoundingly agreed that danger and trauma were ever-present threats in the lives of schoolchildren—especially, but not exclusively, those in the inner city.

Out of these discussions, participants formed a regional crisis committee, which began by establishing three goals: (1) to develop a school crisis intervention model—a general framework from which school districts could establish their own plans and procedures; (2) to train school district personnel to prepare for and respond effectively to crisis situations; and (3) to promote and coordinate emergency mental health services and resources for the region.

Even in its beginning stages, the project proved to be well worth the time and energy invested. Central office administrators and school-based teams in four school districts received training that focused on clinical skills and administrative procedures central to effective crisis response. During the project's first full year of operation, school teams had occasion to implement these skills and procedures more than 40 times, an average of one incident for every two schools. One of these incidents—the near-fatal shooting of a kindergarten student on a school bus caught in gang crossfire—was the object of major media attention.

Based on evidence we compiled on the prevalence of crisis situations and the mediating value of effective preparation and response, we decided to obtain outside funding to continue and expand our committee's efforts as a regional crisis team. The Community Foundation for Greater New Haven and the William Caspar Graustein Memorial Fund agreed to support our work.

This book is a compilation of essential material generated through this collaborative project. It covers (1) the basic assumptions and logic underlying the approach, (2) a general model and practical guidelines to enable schools to prepare for crisis situations, (3) the nuts and bolts of implementing crisis plans in the event of an actual crisis, and (4) sample plans, forms, checklists, and resources to be used in crisis training, preparation, and response.

Scope of the Problem

Although it is true that children have always been exposed to aggression, violence, and loss, the ready availability of firearms and the associated escalating lethality of community violence is altering the nature of this exposure. For black male adolescents and young adults in our country's cities, gun-related murder is now the number one cause of death (American Academy of Pediatrics, 1992). In one study, half the urban high school students surveyed reported knowing someone who was murdered; 37 percent had witnessed a shooting (Pastore, Fisher, and Friedman, 1991). In another study, 20 percent of urban high school students reported that they had been threatened with a gun, while 12 percent had been the target of a shooting (Sheley, McGee, and Wright, 1992). Violence is not only an issue for adolescents and young adults. Parents of seven percent of children younger than age 6 seen in an urban pediatric clinic reported that their child had already witnessed a shooting or stabbing (Taylor, Harik, and Zuckerman, 1992).

The increasing attention given to creating safe schools is a reflection of the growing awareness that schools are a fundamental part of their own communities, and that many of those communities are becoming more and more unsafe. The deteriorating social and economic conditions that have had such a profound effect on family life and community structure have not left school communities untouched. Schools find themselves left to deal with the victims of community violence—the victims of physical trauma, as well as the survivors and witnesses who are unrecognized victims of community violence. More than ever before, schools need to develop and implement effective crisis prevention and response plans to prevent the occurrence of a crisis whenever possible, and to reduce the negative impact of crisis events that do occur.

Basic Assumptions and Key Concepts

The first core assumption underlying the approach in this book is that crisis situations are inevitable in a school setting. Certainly, prevention efforts that deal with school safety and security, as well as those that address personal and emotional needs of students, can go a long way toward reducing the likelihood that a crisis will occur. To the best of our abilities, we can try to make schools into oases—safe, orderly, predictable places that serve the educational needs of children.

Unfortunately, there are humbling limits to what we, as educators, can control, and the extent to which we, as parents and responsible adults, can keep children safe and secure. We live in a world in which natural disasters, life-threatening diseases, and the brutal effects of human violence are endemic—threats that are increasingly apparent.

The second core assumption is that a crisis involves *people* and their personal reactions to the situation. It is not the incident itself that characterizes a crisis situation so much as the reactions that it engenders: alarm, confusion, disorientation, and despair. Dealing with a crisis concerns both the physical and emotional well-being of individuals.

Crisis situations can profoundly affect individuals in the school community. One of the goals of crisis intervention is to minimize the trauma that students, staff, and parents experience. To that end, timing is crucial. A prepared crisis team needs to move quickly to set a tone of compassion and support for the school community.

Many school leaders tend to deal with a crisis by denying, minimizing, or trying to avoid its impact. The reasons for doing so—to maintain a focus on educational goals and to reassure the community that everything is under control—are understandable. However, the net effect of suppressing the reactions of students and teachers can work at cross-purposes to the goals of education. Suppression may cause individuals to take longer to work through their personal reactions to the crisis and they may do so less successfully than if they are allowed to express emotions. If school leaders prolong or thwart the responses to a crisis, students and teachers become less available for learning and for teaching. Consequently, they may feel less safe and more alienated in the school environment.

These key concepts further define the foundation upon which we base our approach to crisis response:

Preparation is absolutely essential to ensure effective response to a school crisis. It is not sufficient to distribute impressive guides on crisis procedures and recommended practices. Responsible individuals must keep crisis plans and materials in a state of readiness, must know what to do and what others will be doing, and must be able to carry out their specific responsibilities under dire circumstances. To conduct the necessary training and planning, school personnel must accept the fact that crises are inevitable. The issue is not whether a crisis will occur, but when it will occur, how serious it will be, and what the response should be.

Being prepared for a crisis is very different from being crisis-oriented. For the beleaguered school administrator, an atmosphere of continual crisis makes it difficult to prepare for—let alone, prevent—the more serious crisis that may lie ahead. Difficult as it may be for administrators to invest time in hypothetical situations, it is crucial that they do so.

There is no ideal crisis preparation and response plan that will work best in all schools and school districts. Crisis preparation and response procedures must be variable and flexible, in recognition of the differences among communities and among schools. Rather than an ideal one-size-fits-all formula, what we present is a general model that school districts can adapt to their unique needs and characteristics.

Central to this model is the use of three distinct crisis teams at the school, district, and regional levels. These teams serve interrelated functions in a coordinated crisis plan. A school system can customize the specific functions of these teams and the relationship among them to fit their needs. For example, smaller school districts may rely more on the district team as the primary line of defense, given the demands of having every school (including those that rarely see a crisis) in an advanced state of readiness. An urban school district or a large, comprehensive high school may place greater emphasis on the school-based team. In a rural community with fewer resources and an interconnected social network, the regional crisis team might take the lead role.

To whatever extent feasible, every school should develop the capacity to deal with crisis situations. There are distinct advantages to empowering those who work with students. Building personnel, who work closely with students, parents, and the school community, are best able to provide direction and support in times of crisis. A school-based team can react quickly, respond in a personal and individualized manner, and continuously monitor the residual effects of a crisis. Also, given the professional background and experience of most educators, school-based teams can achieve the necessary level of preparedness with a modicum of training and planning. Making maximum use of school-based personnel offers distinct advantages over a SWAT team of outside specialists, not the least of which is the message it sends the community that the school is capable of handling serious challenges and caring for children.

Crisis response is just one component in the overall constellation of mental health and social development efforts within

the school community. The overall strategy for crisis response is most effective when it is part of an integrated support system that includes prevention, intervention, and postvention (i.e., reaction to an urgent or crisis situation). Trauma, danger, death, and loss are part of the fabric of life. The skills that enable students to cope with these challenges and setbacks will serve them well throughout life. What is schooling about, after all, if not preparation for life?

As educators, we protect schoolchildren the best we can, but we must also be prepared for unthinkable and unfortunate incidents. When a crisis does occur, we serve children best by recognizing and responding to their psychological needs. Responding to their needs helps to restore their availability for learning and to enhance their coping skills and social development.

2

THE CRISIS
INTERVENTION MODEL

WE DO NOT PROPOSE THIS SCHOOL CRISIS INTERVENTION MODEL AS A universally applicable formula. It is a framework that each school, district, and region can use as a basis for collaboration, adaptation, and expansion to meet its particular needs.

Advantages of a Team Approach

A team approach to crisis response benefits all parties of a school community. Students may need practical assistance, information, emotional support, clinical services, and reinforcement of coping skills during a crisis. They can benefit greatly from the help and support of responsible adults.

Staff members similarly benefit from the information and support that a team can provide. Team members, confronted with the pressures of crisis work, can offer relief or moral support to one another, or may receive such assistance from a district team. In addition, parents develop closer ties to the school and can assist in unique ways, for example, by mobilizing community response or following up after school hours with students identified by school staff as being particularly vulnerable.

The greatest beneficiary of a team approach, however, is the school administrator, who bears a weighty responsibility for major decisions affecting the school (Lichtenstein, Schonfeld, and Kline, 1994). There is no test of leadership quite like a crisis. In times of crisis, an organization or community looks to a leader to restore order and to protect individuals in need. As the philosopher Thomas Hobbes argued, the threat of life-endangering situations is the very basis for investing ultimate authority in an individual.

Despite the need for a leader, we do not endorse an autocratic approach in which all decisions emanate from central command. Quite the contrary, a major crisis calls for a particular style of leadership, a take-charge manner combined with effective teamwork and delegation of vital operations.

Sharing this responsibility with a team offers the administrator some relief from bearing the burden and pressures of the crisis alone. A team approach also enables the administrator to consider multiple vantage points, ideally with the result of finding a reasonable balance among competing priorities such as maximizing order and security, providing accurate information to the school community, and promoting emotional coping and recovery.

Most important, sharing responsibilities among a team is the best assurance that the administration and staff will be able to manage the extreme demands of a crisis well. In a serious crisis, there are too many things happening at once for a single individual to handle them personally, or even to delegate effectively.

The process of collaboration also fosters increased communication between administration and staff, making it more likely that the community and staff will know about, understand, and respect the principal's efforts. The trust that ensues from a team approach can enhance staff morale in ways that extend beyond the life of the crisis.

Determining Which Crises Require a Team Response

Although each team needs to arrive at its own definition of appropriate crises for team response, we suggest that the definition include the following broad categories of situations:

- Bereavement caused by the death of a student, staff, or community member that affects a significant segment of the school population;

- A major environmental crisis such as a flood or fire; and

- Threats to the physical safety of students, such as gun-fire in the school, the taking of hostages, a school bus accident, or the collapse of bleachers causing multiple injuries.

We encourage each team to further develop its own programs to allow incorporation and integration of responses for secondary and impending losses. Many losses, some of which may not be as acute or obvious as those listed, may still have a major impact on one or more students in the school setting. Each team needs to determine its response plan for these scenarios, ranging from an immediate full-team response, to alternative supportive or counseling approaches (e.g., working with select students on a specific issue).

Crisis intervention teams need to work closely with individuals and groups coordinating preventive mental health and counseling services within the school. In the absence of such individuals or groups, the crisis intervention team may wish to assume some portion of this role.

The crisis intervention model represents a proposed organizational structure for school-based crisis intervention. The nature of response will vary widely, depending on the characteristics of the crisis (e.g., response to a student's suicide versus response to the death of a student's parent from natural causes) and the particular setting.

A Systemwide Model

We recommend three levels of organization for a crisis intervention program to work systemwide.

1. Regional Resource Group. A group of individuals, identified at the regional level, assumes the role of providing expert consultation and training to individual school districts. This group also oversees resource needs for the region and coordinates communication among various school districts regarding training and community services. The regional resource group should meet on a regular basis, perhaps three to four times per year.

2. District Crisis Team. Each school district should appoint at least one individual, such as the Director of Pupil Personnel or her designee, to oversee and coordinate crisis intervention services at the district level. Large school districts should consider establishing a district crisis intervention team. This individual or team serves as liaison between the regional resource group and the individual school-based crisis teams, establishes relevant districtwide policy regarding crisis intervention, and adapts program models and recommendations of the regional resource group so that they are consistent with district policies and needs. The team should meet on a regular basis.

3. School-Based Crisis Team. Each school needs to identify appropriate members for their school-based crisis team, under guidelines established by the district crisis team. Though the

makeup of school teams may vary, each school should consider the following staff as potential team members: (a) principal or assistant principal, (b) school nurse or physician, (c)
school social worker, (d) school psychologist, (e) counselor, (f)
secretary, (g) school security personnel, and (h) at least one
teacher. In addition, if the team deems it appropriate, the
school's parent-teacher organization should identify a parent
liaison.

The principal's office and the district crisis team both need a
list of the names, phone numbers, and addresses of members
of the school team and their respective roles. Each school
team should update its roster of team membership at least
yearly. The team should conduct regularly scheduled meetings
throughout the school year, in addition to emergency meetings in response to individual crises.

Roles of School-Based
Crisis Team Members

Members of school-based crisis teams serve in specific roles,
following guidelines established by the district crisis team. An
individual team member may assume multiple roles, or several members may share a particular responsibility, with one
team member designated as primary.

The **Crisis Team Chair,** appointed by an administrator at the
school, is responsible for chairing all scheduled and emergency meetings of the crisis team, overseeing the broad and

specific functioning of the team and its members, ensuring that team members assume all the necessary roles, and communicating directly with the district crisis team.

The **Crisis Team Assistant Chair** (or co-chair), also appointed by an administrator at the school, is responsible for assisting the chair in all functions, and substituting for the chair in the event of his unavailability.

The **Coordinator of Counseling Services,** appointed by the chair, is a team member with appropriate counseling experience. She is responsible for determining, along with the school crisis team, the extent and nature of counseling services indicated by a particular crisis. She is directly responsible for mobilizing community resources if the school is unable to provide the needed direct services, beginning by contacting her counterpart on the district crisis team.

She is also responsible for ensuring that team members receive training in and supervision of the clinical services they provide, and for establishing the mechanisms for providing direct mental health services to students at the time of a crisis. For example, if the crisis team decides to use support rooms to provide service delivery, the Coordinator of Counseling Services needs to organize a system for assigning counselors to staff these rooms.

The Coordinator of Counseling Services oversees approval of students who request to check out of school, as well as those whom staff send home during a crisis or a crisis response.

Finally, she is responsible for reviewing the community resource list provided by the district team's Coordinator of Counseling Services, adding local school resources to the list, and establishing ongoing liaisons with selected sites.

The **Media Coordinator,** preferably a member of the school administration who is appointed by the Chair, is responsible for all contact with the media. School staff should direct all inquiries from representatives of the media to this individual. This is a crucial point that the Chair must stress to all school staff. The Media Coordinator works in close cooperation with his counterpart on the district crisis team. The Media Coordinator prepares a brief press release if indicated, and prepares appropriate statements in collaboration with the Chair of the school crisis team for staff, student, and parent notifications. If time permits, the full team reviews and approves press releases and statements.

The Media Coordinator also prepares a statement to be read to all parents who call the school for further information. The Chair is ultimately responsible for ensuring that the statement is consistent with the wishes of the victim or family members regarding sharing information and that it respects their rights to confidentiality. The Media Coordinator continually updates the statements as further information becomes available (e.g., the time of a funeral or memorial service).

A District Media Coordinator should handle any media interactions beyond the initial brief press release, allowing the school to respond to the needs of its staff and students with the least external interference. The District Media Coordinator should provide all media with a carefully worded press release to ensure that reports of the crisis are accurate and handled responsibly. For example, if a suicide occurs, the District Media Coordinator should inform the media of the need to avoid romanticizing the suicide or denigrating the victim, as well as the need to refer to signs of suicidal risk and to identify regional resources for individuals felt to be at risk for suicide.

The **Staff Notification Coordinator** is responsible for establishing, coordinating, and initiating the telephone tree for notification of team members and other school staff after school hours if needed. She needs to maintain an accurate and up-to-date telephone listing of all school staff.

The **Communications Coordinator** should be the school secretary or other individual ordinarily responsible for answering the telephones. He is responsible for conducting all direct in-house communication. The crisis team will provide him with a brief prepared statement to read to parents calling for information. He screens all incoming calls and maintains a log of telephone calls related to the crisis. He also assists the staff notification coordinator in her role and helps to maintain an accurate telephone listing of community resources and district staff.

The **Crowd Management Coordinator** is responsible for planning mechanisms for crowd management in the event of various potential crises, and for directly supervising the movement of students and staff if such plans are initiated. At the time of the crisis, she assigns one public space monitor for each indoor and outdoor area where students gather, and for each bank of telephones. She also implements and monitors any special dismissal procedures that may be necessary.

The school crisis team should work with the local police and fire departments in establishing a crowd control plan, which is unique to each school. The team should also review the fire evacuation plan to make sure it is current and appropriate for other emergency evacuations. It is essential that the police department designate a school liaison to be on call at all times.

The crowd control plan must include arrangements to cordon off areas that contain physical evidence, assemble students and faculty for presentations, and, in the event of an actual threat to the physical safety of students, ensure the safe and organized movement of students. For example, in response to a sniper in the school, the crisis team must have a means of preventing the dispersion of students, similar to a coordinated evacuation plan in the event of fire. The team also needs to consider unique situations that may occur and develop a plan that can be used to respond to them, such as an accident either involving or being witnessed by a busload of students before or after school hours.

Monitors designated by the Crowd Management Coordinator should provide an informal presence, keeping an eye out for students showing signs of distress. (Monitors may be able to perform regular job tasks while monitoring their designated areas.) Monitors should not play the role of security guards, listen in on conversations, or hover near groups of students. Aggressive intervention or observation may make students feel that monitors are spying on them, which discourages students from displaying their feelings openly with peers and staff. The Crowd Management Coordinator should therefore not assign police officers or security guards to this role. Monitors should also restrict access of media personnel, referring those individuals to the Media Coordinator.

Implementation Guidelines

The intent of this crisis intervention model is to provide schools with an organized, systematic, and flexible approach to responding to a crisis. Each school needs to adapt the guidelines to suit its unique contingencies. Such adaptations, though, should not result in loss of organization or structure that might compromise the success of a team approach to crisis intervention; the district crisis team should ensure that all adaptations preserve the intent of these guidelines.

Notification

Any staff member or community member who is aware of a potential crisis situation should directly contact the Chair or, if he is unavailable, the Assistant Chair of the school crisis team. It is highly desirable to establish an ongoing relationship with the local or regional police for the purpose of both notification and coordination of services. The Chair is responsible for determining whether to notify all or select school crisis team members and additional school staff. The Chair is also responsible for contacting the district crisis team.

The Staff Notification Coordinator coordinates telephone notification through a telephone tree. The purpose of telephone notification is to provide a brief summary of the situation and to communicate the time and location of an emergency team or staff meeting. It is preferable to hold at least a brief staff meeting before the next school day. If notification occurs during the school day, it is best to use the next practical time during the school day for this purpose. Any situation requiring team notification should result in an emergency school crisis team meeting—if possible, prior to any emergency staff meeting.

Agenda of Staff Meeting. The emergency mandatory staff meeting serves the following purposes:

- Allows the crisis team to share all information known about the crisis and the response of the school and community to date, as well as to receive information from the school staff (e.g., feedback about the students' reactions thus far, or input about how their students may respond to the crisis);

- Allows distribution of announcements and discussion of plans for notifying students and parents;

- Enables staff to ask questions and voice their concerns;

- Allows school crisis team members to offer support and assistance directly to staff members (e.g., helping with the notification of students if staff feel deeply affected by the crisis and unable to carry out this task without assistance);

- Reminds the school staff of the crisis intervention model; and

- Outlines pertinent plans of crisis intervention implementation (e.g., if the school will use support rooms) and reviews any procedural accommodations (e.g., school schedule changes).

During this emergency meeting, the staff should schedule a follow-up staff meeting to be held as soon as possible, preferably within 24 hours. The purpose of the follow-up meeting is to provide further information to staff (i.e., clarification of details of the crisis, rumor control, plans for funeral attendance), allow sharing of responses to the immediate crisis intervention, make modifications in crisis intervention plans, and perhaps most critically, offer support and assistance to those staff providing direct services to students. The follow-up meeting should not attempt to offer any premature resolution or closure to the crisis. Additional follow-up staff and crisis team meetings should be held at a suitable later date (typically, two to six weeks following the crisis) to review the team's and the school's response to the crisis, assess what ongoing services are needed, and allow for constructive revisions in the school's response plan.

Contact with the Victim or Family Members. The Crisis Team Chair (or designee) should contact the victim or family members as soon as possible to offer support and assistance. During this contact, the Chair should ascertain what information the victim or family wishes shared with students, staff, and the media. The Chair should verify and clarify the information as indicated and establish ongoing support to the family. In this way, the team can also maintain accurate information (e.g., about funeral plans).

Announcement to Students. The crisis team prepares a written statement regarding the crisis and distributes it to school staff during the emergency staff meeting. Classroom teachers should read this statement to the students at a designated time, for example, during homeroom or first period. The crowd management plan might include special arrangements to ensure that all students are in their classrooms prior to the reading of the announcement. For those teachers who feel unable to read the announcement, the crisis team should offer their support for this purpose. (See Appendix B for sample notification letters.)

Announcement to Parents. The team should prepare a written statement for the Communications Coordinator to read to any parent calling for information. In addition, the Communications Coordinator should prepare a written statement with additional information for distribution to students at the end of the school day. She should prepare samples of these statements in advance and arrange for translation into different languages as needed.

School Routines and Class Activities

Whenever possible, the administration should avoid making major alterations in the school day. Canceling school or dismissing students early is generally inadvisable. Nevertheless, staff should establish a standard procedure for the proper release of students to authorized individuals, as parents may insist on removing their children from school.

Teachers should continue to conduct regularly scheduled classes but need to alter the content of lessons (e.g., postponing tests, allowing discussion of the crisis) to be sensitive to the needs of the students. During the emergency staff meeting, the crisis team should provide teachers with suggestions on how to deal with this and other relevant issues. Teachers should permit students who are unable to continue with their regularly scheduled school day to seek counseling or support services through the support rooms. The administration should make plans that allow interested students and staff to attend funeral or memorial services.

In the event of a teacher's death, another teacher who is known to the students and who is able to respond to their acute grief is the best person to cover the classes of the deceased staff member, at least initially. A member of the school crisis team may be suitable to serve or assist in this role. A substitute or a less familiar teacher may be assigned later.

In the event of a student's death, office staff should try to intercept routine mailings that might automatically be sent to the student or the student's parents.

Support Rooms

The Coordinator of Counseling Services is responsible for ensuring that qualified counseling personnel adequately staff the support rooms, obtaining additional staff through the district crisis team if necessary. The Coordinator of Counseling Services from the district crisis team might serve the critical role of coordinating triage of students referred for counseling services, thus enabling school-based counseling staff to provide direct services to students. Figure 2.1 summarizes the principles of triage.

Each school needs to establish guidelines for sending students to and from the support rooms. Gender-specific rooms may be appropriate at certain elementary school grade levels. The counselor staffing the support room needs to clear all children for return to class, while the Coordinator of Counseling Services needs to oversee clearing any student who is sent home from school, discharging the student only to a parent or guardian. Students reporting to the support room need to return to their scheduled class before the end of the class period. In cases where the student does not return to class, the school should establish a mechanism for notifying the classroom teacher, such as a note sent with another student. Each crisis team should clearly delineate guidelines for contacting parents of students who visit the support rooms.

Memorialization

In cases of the death of a student or staff member, the crisis team should plan a formalized response by the school or

24

— *FIGURE 2.1* —

PRINCIPLES OF TRIAGE FOR STUDENTS IN CRISIS

Students with emergent mental health needs—that is, needs that demand immediate action—should be directly referred to appropriate community resources and should not undergo extensive evaluations or receive extensive counseling services in the school setting prior to referral. It is imperative that the counseling staff identify appropriate emergent services (provided immediately) and urgent services (provided within 48 hours) in the community for this purpose. Sending large numbers of students to such sites as hospital emergency rooms to rule out suicidal risk is not an appropriate response plan. Identifying students with emergent mental health needs, such as those assessed as potentially suicidal, is a central role of the counseling staff. The staff may identify students as in need of evaluation by the nature of the circumstances of the crisis (e.g., if the student was a direct witness to the crisis or a close friend of the victim) or by their reactions upon notification (such as an exaggerated or atypical response).

Students assessed as not being in need of emergent mental health services may be offered limited immediate interventions, perhaps in a group setting. Establishment of support groups, which might continue to meet on an ongoing basis, may be a useful outcome of the support rooms.

Evaluations should be brief and goal specific, the aim being to assign students to one of the two groups (identified as either having emergent mental health needs or needing limited immediate intervention). The counseling staff should defer more lengthy evaluation and services until a later time—for example, the next school day.

subgroup (e.g., the class of the deceased child) that allows students and staff to memorialize the deceased individual at an appropriate time. Memorialization is not meant to signify a formal service or assembly; rather, it may include such activities as planting a tree or establishing a memorial scholarship.

The timing of the memorialization requires careful thought. The crisis team should resist the inclination to plan the memorialization too early in the mourning process. Schools often feel pressured to impose closure on a crisis by initiating a formal memorialization soon after the death. Such a premature action may compel the school to return to its normal routine at the expense of suppressing the grief response.

Immediate issues may include how to formally convey the class's condolences to family survivors or what to do with the child's desk. Each class is likely to deal with the desk in a different way. One class chose to recognize the deceased child's interest in reading by moving the desk to the back of the room and placing library books on it, designating it as a place for quiet reading. Another class chose to remove all belongings from their desks and had the custodial staff clean and reorganize the desks one night, so that the deceased child's desk could anonymously remain in the classroom. The staff can plan other activities such as planting a tree or establishing a memorial scholarship at a later date, months after the death.

We recommend that some means of memorialization occur after the death of a student or staff member, but we discourage activities such as parties, permanent plaques on display in the school, or sections dedicated in school yearbooks, despite good intentions. In the case of suicide, the staff should be careful to avoid excessive glorification of the deceased. (See the section on suicide that follows.) Members of the staff and student body should actively participate in planning the memorialization.

Follow-Up

Crisis teams must acknowledge that children continue to react to a crisis over time. Brief, time-limited interventions without plans for continued and long-term services for those children in need are inadequate. Follow-up is one of the most crucial elements of a crisis intervention program and is particularly well-suited to a school-based model.

Although some community resources may provide long-term counseling, the school crisis team should monitor and facilitate the delivery of long-term services for individual students and should watch out for students who demonstrate the need for services in the aftermath of a crisis. School-based support groups are one possible model of ongoing support services for appropriate students. In general, the follow-up meeting for staff, as discussed earlier, can address some of these concerns.

In addition to regular school crisis team meetings to evaluate the school's response to the crisis and consider modifications in the crisis plan, the team may need a debriefing session in which team members can process their own reactions to the crisis and their response efforts. The district crisis team might supervise such a debriefing. In the event that the crisis involves the entire district or multiple districts—for example, response to a war or environmental disaster—the regional resource group might assume this role. Such meetings not only address the needs of team members (helping the helper), but facilitate communication among team members at the school and district levels and allow crisis team personnel and district plans to benefit from firsthand learning experiences.

Special Issues Concerning Suicide

The principles of school-based crisis intervention in the event of a suicide follow those of the general model, with the additional specific goals of preventing imitative suicides and suicide attempts, and addressing maladaptive responses such as isolation and unwarranted guilt or scapegoating. This section outlines components of the model relevant to addressing suicide attempts, completed suicides, and clusters of suicidal behavior occurring in or impinging on the school community.

General Considerations

Although the factors that promote imitative suicide behavior are not well understood, glamorizing the victim, romanticizing the suicide act, and sensational reporting appear to be significant contributors. The overall school response to a suicide or suicide attempt should minimize these elements, while conveying empathy for the victim and enabling timely dissemination of appropriate information.

The Role of the Media

In cooperation with the local print and electronic media, the crisis team should develop, in advance, guidelines concerning the reporting of suicide. These should address such items as avoiding sensational reporting (e.g., front-page and headline treatment, photos of the deceased, or emotional interviews with friends and relatives); omitting overly detailed accounts of the mechanics and location of the suicide; and discouraging reporters from besieging students or staff on school grounds.

Crisis teams may best accomplish such advance planning on the district or regional level, in collaboration with editors and station managers. It is also advisable to identify preferred content for newspaper articles and broadcasts, such as alternative means of coping, the importance of open communication in preventing suicide, and the availability of resources.

Obtaining Accurate Information

A designated member of the crisis team should be in contact with the police and other authorities to obtain accurate information. She should contact the family to offer condolences and support and to obtain any information the family wishes to make known, including arrangements for the funeral and visitation. The crisis team and school staff should maintain surveillance for secondary cases of suicide or attempted suicide through contacts with appropriate police, medical, and mental health agencies.

Implementating the Plan

The scope of interventions required vary and should be appropriate to the situation and setting. For example, a suicide attempt of low lethality may warrant dealing only with the student's family, immediate circle of friends, and teachers. In contrast, the suicide of a student or staff member usually warrants a broader response. A series of suicides or serious attempts indicates a need for schoolwide intervention.

Disseminating Information

Notification should follow the general guidelines, including advance notification of teaching staff and informing students in small groups, with the opportunity for follow-up discussion. The school staff should couple the announcement with (1) information regarding the availability and location of in-school and community counseling and support resources (e.g., support rooms or suicide hotlines) for students who wish to talk further, and (2) encouragement to make use of these resources.

Case-Finding and Triage

As part of the school's overall suicide prevention planning, the crisis team should sensitize staff and parents to potential suicide risk factors and warning symptoms. In the event of a suicide, the team should alert staff to watch for such symptoms or signs of undue upset, especially in those students who were close to the victim or likely to identify themselves with the victim. Staff should report concerns about specific students or groups of students to the Coordinator of Counseling Services.

Legitimizing Help

The school staff should make efforts to legitimize and destigmatize students' need for help and their communication in asking for help. Staff should contact close friends and other high-risk students in a low-key manner and present the contact as part of the school's routine procedure for dealing with such situations.

Addressing Scapegoating and Romanticization

Staff should be alert to the potential hazards of romanticizing the suicide or scapegoating the victim or other individuals. It is important to discourage the portrayal of suicide as a heroic or glamorous way of coping with adverse circumstances. Staff should also avoid the compelling need to find a scapegoat—a family member, boyfriend or girlfriend, teacher, or school administrator—to whom they can assign the blame and guilt that suicide often carries in its wake. Without denigrating the victim or entering into partisan debate, staff should portray suicide as a maladaptive response—a permanent solution to a temporary problem—that neglects better available alternatives.

Memorialization

The crisis team should delay plans for creating or dedicating a memorial to the victim for at least several weeks. They should also carefully consider what would be an appropriate memorialization. Although it is important to respect the wish to remember the victim, the memorial should not reinforce the idea that suicide is a means of achieving fame, esteem, or notoriety.

Environmental Interventions

When one or more suicides or attempts has occurred at a specific public site (e.g., bridge, water tower, garage, scenic overlook), the crisis team or police should consider monitoring the site or restricting public access.

3

ESTABLISHING CRISIS TEAMS

SETTING UP A CRISIS TEAM CAN BE A FAIRLY SIMPLE PROCESS, ONE THAT involves following a logical sequence of steps, as described in Figure 3.1. The initial task is to decide at which level to begin organization. Unless the school system is small, it is more efficient to begin by establishing a regional or district team than school-based crisis teams. The regional or district team should be able to assist any individual school in a crisis while school teams organize themselves and receive training. The regional or district team can also serve the specialized role of coordinating efforts among schools, or throughout the community, in the event of a large-scale crisis. In small rural or isolated communities, it may work best for the regional and district teams to be one and the same.

— FIGURE 3.1 —

STEPS IN IMPLEMENTING A CRISIS TEAM SYSTEM

A. Establish regional and district teams.

1. Establish a regional crisis prevention and response team that will serve as a coordinating and consulting body.

2. Convene a district team to establish crisis response procedures in accordance with school district policies and preferences, and to oversee implementation of these procedures.

3. Develop a standard crisis response model that is suited to school district and community needs (i.e., by adapting the model in Chapter 2 as needed).

4. Train district team members in crisis response and related issues.

B. Develop school teams and school crisis plans.

1. Identify crisis team members in each school.

2. Train school crisis team members in crisis response and related issues.

3. Convene school crisis teams to review school district procedures and assign responsibilities.

4. Have school crisis teams develop written plans for their schools. (See Appendix A for guidelines.)

5. Have school teams assemble a crisis information folder and crisis kit. (See Appendices C and D.)

— *FIGURE 3.1* —

— continued —

C. Disseminate information at the school level to ensure coordination and support.

  1. Brief the entire school staff on crisis response procedures and school plans.

  2. Inform parent and community service providers about the existence of the team, its function, and its members.

  3. Offer training for all school staff about crisis response and related issues.

D. Arrange for continuing and advanced preparation.

  1. Review procedures periodically and update as needed.

  2. Establish a collection of resource materials in each school to help students, parents, and staff with various kinds of crises.

  3. Provide periodic training to school crisis teams to ensure preparedness, promote team-building, maintain cohesion, enhance skills, and integrate new team members.

  4. Conduct crisis drills at each school, preferably on an annual basis.

  5. Arrange advanced training for school crisis team members—for example, disaster preparedness through the local civil defense organization.

Connections with Support Services

Crisis teams cannot function in isolation from the community. They need to engage relevant agencies to assist with crisis team formation, training, and maintenance. Potential participants in this process include health providers, mental health providers, social services agencies (including youth service bureau and local coordinating council), police, media representatives, parent groups, and clergy.

If a school district or school makes standing arrangements for a particular agency to provide support in the event of a crisis, a representative of that agency should serve on the crisis team. Also, during the process of setting up a crisis team system, the team may identify gaps in service delivery. Identifying a gap should result in plans for narrowing those gaps.

Team Membership

The school principal should always be a member of the school crisis team, typically serving as the Chair or Assistant Chair. Other potential members are listed within the initial description of the school crisis team in Chapter 2.

Itinerant support staff such as school psychologists and social workers should be active members of the school crisis team, despite the fact that they may not be physically present at the school on a full-time basis. They can be valuable contributors to the planning process, providing useful insights on school climate and how it might be modified to increase school safety and help students cope with difficulties and crises. In the event of a crisis, they can be dispatched to the school.

The desirability of including the many individuals who might be valuable team members should be balanced by the need to have a well-functioning and cohesive team. It is important to have enough members so that the absence of any one or two members does not incapacitate the team. Specifically, there should be a team member who is capable of serving as back-up for every critical role. There is a valid concern that the team may become too large, however, resulting in unwieldy team process and diffusion of team members' sense of responsibility. Group dynamics can also bog down with a large team, resulting in inefficiency or reduced participation of individuals. Pitcher and Poland (1992) recommend an upper limit of eight members, although a large school might have good reason to exceed this limit. With too few members, a team runs the risk of gaps in coverage and failing to have important perspectives represented.

Relationship to Other School Teams

Although the membership of crisis teams often overlaps with that of other school teams (e.g., student assistance team, child study team, mental health team), the function and the membership should be differentiated from other teams. Crisis response should not be an additional responsibility of a team that exists for some other purpose.

Similarly, the role of the crisis team should be specific to crisis prevention and response. The team should not serve functions related to academic, advising, or special education missions, nor should it follow the mental health issues of individuals beyond those related to a specific crisis. The crisis team avoids duplication of services by referring to, or coordinating with, existing support services. When keeping to their specific and limited role of handling events of utmost urgency, crisis teams tend to meet with little resistance compared with other quasi-educational programs and services.

Staff Development

Experience indicates that crisis teams cannot serve their purpose without sufficient training. A minimum of a full day of training for the entire team is essential, and a half day or more of follow-up is recommended. Our experience suggests that the ideal amount of time is from 12 to 15 hours.

Successful training must focus on both content and process. Recommended content areas include

- An overview of crisis theory and its implications for school settings;

- The concepts of loss and grief;

- Developmental issues in children's response to death and loss; and

- Responses to specific kinds of crises—suicide, homicide, and other crises relevant to the school or community.

Training components designed to address team process may include

- Team-building exercises, especially those that encourage self-examination of personal strengths and sensitivities relevant to crisis response;

- Simulation exercises in which team members apply the model, practice assigned roles, and challenge ineffective team functioning; and

- A question-and-answer period with a panel of school personnel who have managed a crisis in the recent past, plus select community resource persons.

A key part of the training is to have teams work through simulated crisis events. Vignettes for this purpose are provided in Appendix E. Each situation presents some new wrinkle in the timing or nature of the crisis event and raises questions that have no clear right or wrong answers. Teams need to think productively about the "what ifs" and practice reaching decisions in the absence of certainty.

Challenges and Strategies

Despite the compelling reasons for establishing crisis teams and the general support voiced by the community and school staff alike, administrators who wish to implement a crisis response structure face several challenges:

- Ensuring sufficient time and resources to train a crisis team and to develop district plans and procedures;

- Ensuring that individual schools establish teams, adapt district plans to suit their needs, and maintain a state of readiness between crises;

- Sensitizing all administrators to the importance of addressing children's emotional and psychosocial needs in the event of a crisis, as well as those of staff members;

- Encouraging administrators to share decision-making and crisis-related responsibilities with the team; and

- Persuading a school system to maintain crisis response planning, training, and services as a high priority. (Once the team is functioning well, it is tempting to pull back the resources that have supported it.)

Although there is no panacea that guarantees success, the following strategies can maximize a team's likelihood of achieving its goals for crisis preparation and response.

District Support

It is crucial at the outset that those promoting a crisis intervention plan convince the superintendent, other high-ranking district-level administrators, and the school board of its importance. Likewise, administrators and board members need to understand what is involved in terms of training and personnel time needed to prepare the team.

Building Support

Building administrators need a sound understanding of the rationale for having a school-based crisis team. They must demonstrate their commitment through personal involvement on the team and by providing adequately for training needs and periodic self-monitoring.

Ensuring the support of building administrators throughout a school district may require a concerted carrot-and-stick approach that includes convincing school administrators of the importance of crisis preparation, making adequate training and resources available, specifying clearly what is expected of them, and monitoring school-based efforts on a regular basis. We recommend annual monitoring of school crisis plans to ensure an ongoing state of preparedness by school crisis teams.

Training

High-quality training is the most effective antidote to most problems that arise. It helps to ensure that team members are motivated and confident, that they have completed protocols and developed necessary skills, and that team interactions have evolved to a high level of functioning. It also offers an opportunity to sensitize school personnel to the effects of trauma and other psychosocial stressors.

Trainers must allot ample time, preferably with multiple training sessions or training followed by coaching, for effective training (as opposed to a one-shot approach that risks information overload). Trainers can increase participants' motivation to learn about crisis response by stressing the likelihood that a crisis will occur and the importance of the roles the team will assume. The training plan should include repeat presentations in subsequent years to train new staff and offer a review for previously trained personnel.

Practice

A well-conceived training plan addresses the possibility that the crisis plan may not be precisely executed under the duress of an actual crisis. The key is to apply a basic principle of learning: the best preparation occurs under conditions that most closely approximate real-life applications. Reading and discussing issues in crisis intervention are certainly of value, but readiness improves greatly by talking through a simulation exercise or, even better, by rehearsing in the form of a crisis drill. A training sequence that combines all of these techniques approaches the ideal.

Given the obstacles described here, some schools choose to prepare themselves more adequately than others. Although a similarly high level of preparedness at all schools is the goal, expecting and demanding uniformity is not without costs. It may be counterproductive to establish optimal, but unrealistic, standards that seem overwhelming to some schools. On the other hand, setting realistic minimum standards should not serve to discourage those schools with a greater interest in and need for crisis preparation (such as large high schools) from taking additional steps.

One approach is to break down the long-term process of establishing school-based crisis teams into several separate stages. The steps outlined in Figure 3.1 (pp. 34–35) might be used for this purpose. Each year, the district crisis team can raise the minimum standards for each school team to a successively higher level. More advanced teams can accelerate their efforts toward achieving total preparedness, while other school teams proceed more slowly and adhere to the minimum standards. Such a system of evolving standards should compel school personnel to revisit plans and procedures annually and create a sustained interest in follow-up training and resource materials.

Once school crisis teams are established, a recommended practice is to conduct random drills, which enable crisis team members to rehearse their roles in context. Crisis drills provide a wake-up call about the ever-present possibility of crisis, as well as an opportunity to evaluate the adequacy of a

school's crisis plans and response efforts. Drills also let staff
know what to expect and how to respond in the event of a crisis, thus reducing the likelihood that confusion, doubt, or
panic will arise.

Crisis drills may serve to highlight the importance of effective
team process, since drills are apt to reveal the shortcomings of
an autocratic approach. Conversely, the constructive team
dynamics and mutual respect among team members that
emerge during collaborative crisis team preparation are likely
to carry over to an actual crisis.

Even if the school crisis team is well prepared, however, the
district crisis team may make a practice of sending an experienced district crisis team member to assist a school crisis team
with limited experience during a crisis. Although this practice
may seem inconsistent with a model that relies heavily on a
strong and independent school crisis team, feedback from
school personnel in the aftermath of a crisis consistently
reveals that the unobtrusive presence of a known and trusted
observer or expert provides an enormous boost to a school
crisis team, even when the school team handles the situation competently and independently.

4

RESPONDING TO A CRISIS

THREE CHALLENGES COMMONLY ARISE WHEN SCHOOL PERSONNEL respond to a crisis: activation of crisis response plans, coordination and communication, and interaction with the media.

Activating the Crisis Plan

The most common breakdown in school-based crisis response is failure to activate the crisis plan, which may occur when an administrator minimizes or denies the seriousness of a situation. For this reason, school district procedures might include automatic contact with the Chair or Assistant Chair of the district crisis team in the event of a crisis or other situation that might be perceived as a crisis. This contact serves as a check in assessing the seriousness of the situation. This step, perhaps more than any other, may require pointed and repeated reminders from the district crisis team to ensure that building administrators consistently follow this procedure.

Coordination and Communication

Coordination and communication are essential elements in effective crisis management. The first step in this process is to obtain as much factual information as possible from parents, police, or medical personnel. The crisis team uses this information to talk knowledgeably with staff, students, and the media; to squelch inevitable rumors; and to determine the types of response efforts and support services that the school may need in a particular situation. A suicide, for example, calls for a different response than an automobile accident.

A well-trained crisis team can facilitate the coordinated meshing of support functions. The preassigned roles enable crisis team members to function in a way that best meets the needs of the school, while adhering to the school crisis plan and the school district procedures.

Crisis team members should keep in constant communication with each other and with building and central office administrators. Additionally, the school crisis team needs to ensure that the entire faculty is briefed about events, support activities, and follow-up efforts. Scheduling a staff meeting at the first possible opportunity allows the faculty and staff to receive adequate information, to have their questions answered, to ask for assistance, and to feel supported.

It is particularly important that office staff are prepared to respond to questions from parents, media, and other community members. In certain situations, the Media Coordinator may want to provide office staff with a script for responding to telephone inquiries.

Parents may also seek help in coping with a crisis or helping their children cope. Ideally, the school crisis plan should include a way of handling parents' concerns, such as by scheduling a parent information session.

There are so many considerations involved in crisis response coordination and communication that it is a daunting task to ensure that they are all addressed in a timely fashion and logical sequence. A checklist of crisis response procedures, which might serve as a standard protocol for a school district, is an invaluable guide.

Dealing with the Media

Police scanners and citizens band radios have changed the nature of communication about local events. News media regularly monitor these devices to keep informed of potential stories. If the police have responded to a situation involving school-age children, it is likely that the media will not only broadcast it before the police have a chance to fully inform school personnel, but also that the media may appear on the school doorstep before the school crisis team has planned its response.

Advance planning is critical in handling the media. School personnel should be aware of their district's policies with respect to the media. Although the crisis team cannot prevent others from speaking to the media off school property, school policy often bans media representatives from school grounds unless invited. Thus, the crisis team should inform or remind the school community that, on school property, the Media Coordinator handles communications. The crisis team may assign the role of media coordinator, or the central office may handle the role. In some districts, it is the responsibility of a public information officer.

The Media Coordinator's role is to draft press releases, determine times that are appropriate for school personnel to speak to the media, and keep the media informed. It should not be an adversarial relationship. A good relationship with the local media can help immensely in correcting misinformation and notifying the public of response efforts in the school or community. Figure 4.1 provides guidelines for effectively dealing with the media.

In unusual situations such as a kidnapping, death inside a school, or a hostage situation, the media may go so far as to attempt to enter the school to interview or videotape students

— FIGURE 4.1 —

GUIDELINES FOR WORKING WITH THE MEDIA

It is important to place media coverage high on your list of priorities and view it as an asset to your work. The following suggestions can help increase the educational value of media stories surrounding a crisis and minimize the potential emotional damage that inadequate reporting may generate.

1. Set policies and make decisions about media contact before the occurrence of a crisis event.

2. Direct all media inquiries during a crisis to designated spokespersons. This practice avoids confusion and ensures consistency in information given to the media.

3. Insist that no media personnel be allowed on school grounds during school hours. Give media personnel a proposed time and place when you will provide them with information.

4. Use clear, simple, layman's terminology that readers or viewers can understand.

5. Avoid being defensive. Do not treat the interviewer as an adversary. Acknowledge the difficulty of the media's role and take the position of helpfulness. If you do not know the answer to a question, find out and call back, or put the interviewer in contact with another resource.

6. Use caution if the interviewer requests to be put in contact with witnesses, alleged offenders, or survivors. Your first priority is to protect your students and staff and minimize the traumatic effects of the crisis situation on them.

— *FIGURE 4.1* —

— continued —

7. Make clear before being recorded or interviewed live that you do not think it appropriate to discuss specific details of the event, particularly suicide or weapons-related deaths. Avoid sensationalizing. General information is more beneficial.

8. Describe the roles and activities of your crisis team, staff members, and community members who were helpful during crisis response.

9. Do not insist on seeing questions in advance or on editing the final copy. The media will use what fits the purpose, theme, or time frame of their medium. You willingness to be interviewed involves some degree of trust. If you have serious doubts, refer the interviewer to someone else.

Adapted from "Guidelines for Media Interviews," courtesy of the American Association of Suicidology.

and staff. Communication between the Media Coordinator and security personnel is important for ensuring that school staff secure the points of school access and escort media representatives out of the school and off school grounds if necessary.

5

PROVIDING CLINICAL SUPPORT

OUR RATIONALE FOR DEVELOPING A SCHOOL-BASED CRISIS INTERVENTION model is based on well-established evidence that crisis periods represent significant turning points in children's lives. Both children and adults who experience a traumatic event typically respond by entering a state of shock, followed by a longer period of deep upset and emotional disorganization in which prior coping mechanisms often prove inadequate (Halprin, 1973; Rapoport, 1965).

Traumatic events that occur both on and off school grounds may precipitate short-term crisis responses among schoolchildren. These responses are characterized by a range of emotional, behavioral, relational, and academic difficulties. If the school staff does not address the trauma, disruptions in children's concentration can, over time, negatively affect long-term academic progress. Unresolved grief reactions can also contribute to more serious psychological difficulties. Left untended, this unresolved grief can spread throughout the school, contributing to poor morale and school climate.

Although crisis situations do pose psychological threats, they do not necessarily result in negative outcomes. Support, information, and practical assistance can enable a traumatized child to gain new insights, coping skills, relationships, and confidence. Effective interventions in the classroom and at school can foster these types of gains (Klingman, 1988). The ability of significant adults to deal with a traumatic event is a key factor in children's positive recovery from trauma (Lyons, 1987). Thus, it is within the capacity of skilled school personnel to help students exert mastery over a tragic situation. The *School Crisis Survival Guide* (Petersen and Straub, 1992) is one source of therapeutic activities, counseling guidelines, and materials relating to a school crisis.

School staff who are familiar with the students in their building can anticipate students' responses to a particular crisis event based on the students' typical coping mechanisms and adaptive functioning (i.e., how they have dealt with other challenges in the past), their developmental level, and their conceptual understanding of the crisis event. If the crisis involves a death, staff working with the children need to appreciate the developmental process by which children acquire a conceptual understanding of death and how children of various developmental levels respond to the death of others (Schonfeld, 1993; Schonfeld and Kappelman, 1992).

Support and Interventions for Students

At times of crisis, children and adolescents can benefit from specific types of information and support to help them develop mastery in coping with the experience (Schonfeld, 1989). The most broadly applicable types of support services— those directed toward students who handle the crisis with minimal difficulty, who appear to be psychologically intact, and who are able to mobilize adaptive coping mechanisms— can be offered on a large scale, even schoolwide if warranted. Smaller-scale or individual interventions can be offered within limits that are defined by school resources, the overall demands created by the specific crisis situation, and the extent of the individuals' needs. The most intensive and specialized interventions, for those students who are highly traumatized or at risk, typically necessitate referral to community agencies.

The specific range of options selected depends on the nature of the crisis and the resources of the overall crisis response system. What is essential, however, is to ensure a full range of options, from broad-based to specialized. Broad-based support services reduce the level of reliance on scarce and costly services; they also provide opportunities for identifying individuals who demonstrate atypical reactions and additional needs, thus facilitating triage.

Typical supportive and therapeutic options include classroom discussion, brief interventions for identified students, school-based groups for at-risk students, and referral to community resources. Figure 5.1 provides a protocol for determining student service needs and clarifying the clinical decisions to be made within the school setting.

Classroom Discussion

Classroom discussions can have a positive and far-reaching impact on students' abilities to cope. The most readily implemented, and often most effective, approach is for teachers to conduct discussions in their regular classes. The nature and goals of the discussion depend in part on the developmental level of the students, the unique characteristics of the traumatic experience, and the students' immediate needs. Teachers generally prove to be capable of leading such discussions with a modicum of direction and support, such as the information provided by the school crisis team during an initial crisis meeting for all staff. School crisis team members can arrange to assist those teachers who feel they are unable or unwilling to lead this type of class discussion.

Classroom discussion should follow the lead of the students, progressing naturally with as little redirection as possible, thus enabling the teacher to identify the concerns and emotional needs of all students. The teacher should allow discussion to continue as long as students evidence reactions to the crisis such as fear, anxiety, anger, frustration, and sadness. The teacher may feel relief when an intense and productive discussion draws to a close, but the end of the discussion does not necessarily mean that the business at hand is exhausted

— *FIGURE 5.1* —

PROTOCOL FOR DETERMINING STUDENTS' SERVICE NEEDS

1. With certain students who are unaware of the crisis incident, it may be necessary to prepare them individually for classroom discussion because of their relationship with the victim. Examples of students who may benefit from preparation include close friends, fellow students with a special association (e.g., teammates), and relatives.

2. Because of their pre-existing relationships with students, classroom teachers are the best persons to lead classroom discussions.

3. If classroom discussions prove to be inadequate in helping some students manage their emotional reactions to the incident, these students may benefit from services available through a support room.

4. Upon a student's arrival at the support room, the counselor should briefly evaluate him to rule out profound states of disorganization, anxiety, or depression. A student who is profoundly affected by his emotions might benefit from an expedited referral to a local mental health clinic or private practitioner. School staff should contact the student's parent or guardian to transport and accompany the student to these services.

5. Counselors should permit students they have determined to be appropriate for support room services to engage in casual, unstructured conversations with their peers and support

— *FIGURE 5.1* —

— continued —

room staff. A guiding principle is to achieve the greatest benefit to the student with the least intrusive intervention possible.

6. If casual, unstructured conversations prove to be inadequate to meet the student's needs, the counselor should consider structured, goal-directed groups as the next level of intervention. These groups should be sufficiently open to allow students to come and go as their needs are met.

7. Students who continue to exhibit needs following support room contacts on the first day of a crisis should be encouraged to return the following day. These students may also benefit from an ongoing support group.

8. Students who continue to exhibit considerable levels of need beyond those of the general student body (either in time or intensity) should receive individual attention from school support staff. Counselors should monitor these students for needs that may exceed the resources of the school.

9. Throughout the crisis period, school staff should inform parents of any exceptional responses their children make to the crisis.

Courtesy of Scott Newgass, Technical Assistance Coordinator of the School Crisis Response Initiative, National Center for Children Exposed to Violence and resolved. Rather, it may simply signal the need for recovery time. The teacher may discover that the class needs to return to the subject at a later point.

Information that teachers share in this setting helps to dispel rumors, correct misinformation and—especially for younger children—dispel fears based on misconceptions. The teacher should present information clearly and directly but without unnecessary embellishment or excessive detail. She should allow ample time for questions, encouraging (though not forcing) students' questions and answering them honestly.

The teacher may use other types of activities to supplement group discussions, since students may be reluctant to discuss their feelings directly. The use of drawings (for younger students), essays (for older students), or other projective techniques can offer students a vehicle for expressing their feelings and concerns indirectly and privately. In situations where the trauma has not been as immediate or intense, the teacher can use characters or scenes within books and videos to discuss a related event or loss. The similarity of experience may serve to stimulate discussion and provide examples of positive coping.

Classroom discussions are especially useful for normalizing the experience of grief and stress reactions and for helping students identify and seek out supports in their school, home, and community. Although it is useful for students to share personal experiences and feelings, it is necessary, especially at the younger grade levels, to monitor the degree of personal disclosure so as to limit material that is inappropriate for a classroom setting and best kept confidential.

Teachers and other school staff should keep in mind that classroom discussions are not meant to serve as group therapy. The intensity of the discussion should be closely monitored. If it appears to exceed a level useful to the group, the teacher can refocus the discussion on students' experiences, knowledge of adaptive coping techniques (e.g., "What have people done in the past that helped you cope with a loss that may be useful to you in dealing with this experience?"), and ways they might seek out other available sources of support, including their parents.

Brief Therapeutic Interventions

The mental health personnel who staff support rooms can provide relatively brief interventions for students or other members of the school community who require more specialized services. Informal, unstructured conversations with support room staff, either individually or along with peers, are a common and reasonable option. The conversation provides an opportunity for staff to determine whether continued or more intensive services appear needed.

Situations in which several individuals have been exposed to extreme trauma (e.g., witnessing multiple, gruesome deaths) may call for the use of a structured, group debriefing procedure.

Critical incident stress debriefing (CISD), a technique borrowed from the emergency medical field for this specific purpose, may be useful in certain exceptional circumstances. CISD provides support to recently traumatized individuals using a structured, time-limited group session to encourage individuals to talk through their personal experience of, and feelings about, the traumatic event. The goal is to help witnesses and victims mobilize existing coping mechanisms and fend off debilitating symptoms of post-traumatic stress.

CISD includes an educational component of preparing participants to recognize and employ strategies for reducing common stress symptoms. Interaction with others who were exposed to the same trauma helps create a sense of community, thus encouraging participants to accept support from others. It also provides an opportunity to identify individuals who are reacting to the crisis in an extreme or dysfunctional manner—those who need more individualized psychological intervention.

School-Based Groups for At-Risk Students

It is often useful to facilitate small-group discussions of students who are either at risk because of some shared characteristic (e.g., close friends of the victim, or members of a deceased student's athletic team), or who are already demonstrating a pronounced reaction to the traumatic experience. Students who did not know a victim, but who experienced a similar loss previously, may be receptive to new outlets for working through grief following a death in the school community. Groups that come together in support rooms in the immediate aftermath of the crisis event may continue for a period of weeks or months as a more formal peer support group facilitated by a member of the counseling staff.

Referral to Community Resources

Given the limited scope of mental health resources in school settings, staff may become overwhelmed unless they adhere to the principles of triage (Figure 2.1, p. 25) and offer a limited, judicious array of goal-directed evaluation, support, and intervention services. The crisis team should also be alert to the need for follow-up or continued services for specific students or staff in the aftermath of a crisis.

Support for Staff

Crisis planning often overlooks school staff members as a group that needs support during a crisis situation. There is the unspoken expectation that adults should set aside their own feelings and emotional reactions to meet the emergent emotional needs of students. Yet, staff members experience the same types of reactions that students do: shock, denial, anger, fear, and grief. The crisis team needs to promote ways to allow the staff the opportunity to vent feelings of anger and frustration, to be listened to, and to cry. A crisis actually provides the opportunity for staff to provide mutual support in times of stress and to reinforce the bonds that define a caring community.

Staff support can be an important function for a crisis team member who serves as a "floater," moving from room to room to monitor how staff members are doing, as well as assessing the school climate. It may be advisable to designate a space such as the faculty lounge where staff members can go for a few minutes to compose themselves or speak with peers, possibly while the floater covers their class or assignment. If there are additional support personnel in the building who are not working with children, the principal might assign one person to assist in the staff support room.

A staff support room may also be a way to involve parents who want to help. Food is a great calming medium during a stressful situation. The crisis team might ask parents who want to be supportive to bring in doughnuts, juice, fresh fruit, or other goodies for the staff.

Without attention to the needs of the adults in the building, some staff members will have to look after themselves as best they can—perhaps by calling in sick the next day. As staff members themselves struggle, they may feel unable to meet the needs of students who turn to them as familiar, trusted adults who help them understand and cope with a difficult situation. By assisting staff members with their own discomfort, the crisis team can greatly enhance a staff's effectiveness in assisting students.

6

THE OVERALL PICTURE: INTEGRATED MENTAL HEALTH SERVICES

A MAJOR OBSTACLE TO ESTABLISHING A COMPREHENSIVE SYSTEM OF school-based crisis intervention teams is that mental health professionals in schools are scarce and the demands on their time are great. If crisis activities compete with other valuable services for time and resources, this may generate conflicts. But if crisis response is one of several components of an integrated school mental health service system, a crisis response system can be readily established and sustained by effective teamwork and coordinated use of resources.

A coordinated mental health delivery system includes a range of services that span the continuum of approaches from prevention to intervention to reaction (or postvention), as shown in Figure 6.1. An effective system does not focus on one part of the continuum to the exclusion of others, but rather relies

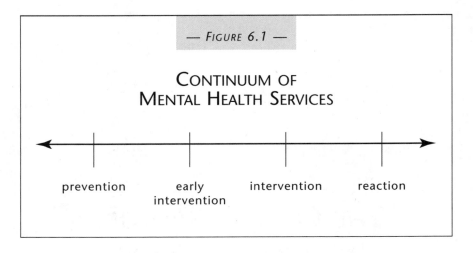

— *FIGURE 6.1* —

CONTINUUM OF MENTAL HEALTH SERVICES

prevention   early   intervention   reaction
intervention

on a thoughtful and strategic mix of approaches that complement one another.

Consider, for example, a high school that incorporates prevention strategies both into curriculum, by teaching life skills (e.g., social problem-solving, communication, conflict resolution, stress reduction), and into guidance, with the assignment of staff advisors to all students. Expected outcomes of such a system include strengthening the bonds between school staff and students, and promoting a positive school climate.

Thus, prevention activities may facilitate crisis response in several ways:

- School staff may be more effective in providing support to students in time of crisis;

- Students may be better able to respond to personal challenges in a mature and adaptive manner, perhaps even to learn and grow from the experience;

- School staff may learn about crisis situations more rapidly and obtain helpful information from students; and

- Students may be less likely to engage in risky or injurious behavior.

An emphasis on prevention does not, however, offer any guarantee that crises will not occur. Prevention activities may actually result in more mental health needs coming to light as students disclose their troubling personal situations to trusted, supportive school personnel. What happens in classrooms on a daily basis is also a significant component of a crisis response system. Teachers build rapport and trust with students as they model appropriate ways of expressing feelings and as they respond attentively and respectfully to important personal issues that find their way into the classroom.

The extent to which students communicate feelings and let their personal needs be known depends on the classroom climate and expectations that teachers establish and nurture. For example, students may learn that they can turn to teachers for accurate and helpful information about death and loss. Discussions on such topics let students know that they can talk about painful subjects with a teacher, thereby setting the foundation for constructive interactions during a crisis.

Returning to the model presented in Figure 6.1, where does crisis response fall along the continuum of mental health services? There is a tendency to characterize crisis response as being strictly in the realm of reaction. In the absence of preparation, that is indeed the case. The approach to crisis response presented in this book, however, incorporates prevention and intervention strategies.

An invisible benefit of managing a crisis effectively is the prevention of complications and catastrophes that may result when crisis response efforts are absent or inept. The most familiar and distressing example of what can result from inadequate crisis response is a contagion effect after a suicide. A crisis can also present the opportunity for students or staff who have been traumatized by other stressors to acknowledge their precarious state and accept outside help.

By being prepared, knowledgeable, and confident in their ability to deal with a crisis situation, the school crisis team prevents further escalation of the crisis as a result of secondary complications and helps students and staff recover. Cooperative and successful crisis intervention by school personnel promotes feelings of pride and empowerment within the school environment, at the same time fostering trust and support from the community.

Promoting school safety is a natural accompaniment to crisis planning. A school crisis team, in considering the kinds of crises that may occur or circumstances that may exacerbate a crisis situation, may suggest various safety measures such as locking school entrances that cannot be monitored, eliminating environmental hazards, and establishing policies to eradicate injurious behavior and the carrying of weapons. It is best to coordinate initiatives to promote safe schools and violence prevention with crisis preparation and response.

A comprehensive safe schools and crisis response initiative may sound commendable and valuable, but may not seem feasible for many school districts. As worsening financial situations require schools to do more with less, the very school districts that need a crisis response system most may be least able to manage it or afford it. These districts may need to explore creative and cost-effective approaches that may include establishing regional or state-level centers that provide an array of services, such as

- Developing training materials,

- Helping school personnel develop crisis plans,

- Serving as a clearinghouse for resource materials and information,

- Providing on-site assistance in the event of a school crisis, and

- Assisting teams with post-event evaluation of crisis response (i.e., debriefing).

It may be possible to develop such centers through existing regional educational collaboratives or to establish new consortium agreements. Alternative possibilities include grants from federal programs (e.g., Safe and Drug Free Schools) or private foundations, or the enactment of new state legislation.

Schools that are safe; that promote open communication among students, staff, and parents; that teach and reinforce personal responsibility and prosocial behavior; that provide support for individuals in crisis—such schools, by being supportive of mental health needs, are also supportive of educational goals. A crisis prevention and response system is a natural part of this picture and further contributes to the sense of well-being and security that prevails in such environments.

Appendix A

Guidelines for Developing a School Crisis Plan

The Crisis Team should review and update the School Crisis Plan annually and discuss it at least briefly with all staff. The plan should include the following information.

☐ The name, physical address, and phone number of the school.

☐ Members of the school crisis team, including room numbers, telephone numbers (if applicable), and itinerant members' schedules. The best place for this information is the front page of the plan.

☐ A staff telephone tree that indicates who calls whom if a crisis occurs after school hours.

☐ An in-school crisis code to convene the team in an emergency. Specify the succession of crisis team members

who are authorized to activate the code when the
principal is out of the building.

☐ A description of the role of each team member. Refer to
the school-based crisis intervention model (Chapter 2)
to define roles.

☐ A list of alternates in case crisis team members are absent.
For example, who covers the telephones if the secretary
is absent.

☐ A list that assigns staff to cover classrooms of teachers
who are involved in crisis management.

☐ A list of staff members who are knowledgeable in first
aid and CPR.

☐ A list of the contents of the school crisis kit and its location.

☐ A neighborhood site to which school staff will evacuate
students in the event of a natural disaster or extreme
emergency. Specify a contact person and telephone number.

☐ Indicate the computer filenames of form letters to serve
as notification to parents or guardians (see Appendix B
for sample).

☐ An outline of expectations for all staff during a crisis
event (e.g., custodians, teachers during planning periods).

APPENDIX B

SAMPLE NOTIFICATION LETTERS

THE FOLLOWING SAMPLE LETTERS ARE TO SEND TO THE DIFFERENT CON-stituents within the school community to ensure that accurate, concise, and consistent information is disseminated to everyone. The information in brackets needs to be selected or filled in appropriately for each situation.

Sample Notice for Staff

This is a sample letter to give to staff immediately following the notice that a member of the school community has died. See page 75 for information pertinent to footnoted brackets.

Date:
To: All Staff
From: [name of school] Crisis Team
Re: [name of deceased][1]

The [sudden] death of [name of deceased][1] [has made OR is expected to make] a major impact on our entire school community. Our crisis team has been mobilized to respond to this tragic event.

On [date], [name of deceased][1] [fact][2]. We can expect a variety of reactions to this loss from our students, parents, and members of our staff. Some reactions may be mild, others may be intense.

To effectively assist all members of our school community, an emergency staff meeting will be held at [time] on [date] in the [designate a place: e.g., cafeteria, auditorium]. At that time, our crisis team will provide further details, including the method of presentation of information to students. In the interim, please refer all inquiries from outside sources to [name of Media or Communications Coordinator].

With students, you may acknowledge that this death has occurred. However, please avoid discussion of details and state simply that school staff will provide information to everyone shortly. If necessary, please refer any student who appears to be in crisis to [name of Coordinator of Counseling Services]. We also encourage staff members to seek assistance from [name of Coordinator of Counseling Services], if desired.

Emergency Staff Meeting
Time:
Date:
Location:

Sample Notice for Students

This is a sample statement that should be given to teachers and other staff to read to students during homeroom or other designated time.

As you may know, on [day, date], [name of deceased][1], [fact][2].

I know many of you will have questions and maybe some upsetting feelings about [name of deceased]'s death. I will try to answer any questions you might have. We will take the remainder of this [period or class] to talk about this if you wish to. It is okay to cry or to feel angry. It is very important that you express your feelings, whatever they may be. If I cannot answer your questions or if you need to talk privately, the [list available support rooms: e.g., guidance office, nurse's office, room 102] [is, are] available now. Anyone who needs to go to a [counselor or support room] may go now. I will write you a pass.

Sample Notice for Parents

Print this notice on school stationery; mail or give to students to take home.

Dear Parent or Guardian:

It is with deep regret that we must inform you of a recent loss to our school. On [day, date], [name of deceased][1] [fact][2]. This loss will undoubtedly raise many questions, concerns, and feelings among our entire school community, particularly our students.

[Name of school or school district] has established a Crisis Intervention Team made up of a variety of professionals trained to respond to the needs of students and parents at a time such as this.

If you would like additional information or need assistance, please contact [name of Communications Coordinator or Coordinator of Counseling Services] at [phone number]. We have enclosed some information that may be useful to you in helping your child at home. At [name of school], we have counselors available for any student who may require assistance. We also encourage parents to use our resources.

Very truly yours,
[signature space]

[type name of signer and title; the notice is generally signed by principal, superintendent, or crisis team chair]

The following footnotes indicate examples of information that may be an appropriate style for filling in footnoted brackets.

[1]John Smith, one of our 8th grade students; Mrs. Smith, who taught 7th grade English; Mr. Jones, Mary Jones's father

[2] was killed in an automobile accident; died after a long illness; died of a sudden stroke; took her own life

APPENDIX C

SAMPLE CONTENTS OF A CRISIS INFORMATION FOLDER

☐ School district crisis procedures.

☐ School crisis plan, including phone tree and phone numbers for district crisis team.

☐ Evacuation map of the building with all room numbers clearly indicated. Mark any doors that are routinely open during the day that may need to be secured.

☐ List of all people regularly in the building, including secretaries, custodians, food-service personnel, aides, volunteers, and parent assistants.

☐ Resource articles on relevant topics (e.g., death, child safety, suicide prevention) that can be given to parents and students, or sent home with notification letters.

☐ Location of student and staff emergency cards (preferably close by).

☐ Blank forms that may be needed in a crisis (e.g., accident report).

☐ Location of crisis kit (see Appendix D) and other emergency materials and equipment.

Appendix D

Sample Contents of a School Crisis Kit

Each school should assemble a kit containing materials and supplies that staff may need in an emergency. The kit should be known and accessible not only to crisis team members, but to any staff member who may need to take initiative in responding to a crisis. The following list of sample contents is adapted from Portis and Portis (1992), which may be consulted for further information on disaster preparedness.

☐ First aid kit

☐ Radio communication system (e.g., walkie-talkie)

☐ Flashlights

☐ Matches

☐ Blankets

☐ Writing supplies, including paper, index cards, markers

☐ Storage materials, such as large plastic bags, plastic water containers, pails

☐ Water purification materials (tablets, iodine, or bleach)

☐ Rope

☐ Knife

☐ Scissors

☐ Hand tools (hammer, small hand saw, screwdriver)

☐ Tape (duct, masking)

Appendix E

Vignettes for Crisis Team Training

As a core component of crisis team training, it is especially helpful to conduct simulation exercises. Using the vignettes that follow, a facilitator can guide the discussion by posing a series of questions and providing additional information. As an illustration, we have provided a facilitator's guide for Vignette D.

To be effective, the vignettes used should simulate an actual crisis event. In dealing with the hypothetical event, team members adopt the crisis team roles that are outlined in this book and introduced during training. During the exercise, it is important to have participants stay in role and on task. The facilitators should have the crisis evolve over time, just as in real life. Sometimes new challenges arise just as participants think they are addressing a problem effectively. Although this may cause anxiety for participants, figuring out how to work productively as a team under pressure is a major goal of the activity.

The facilitator should choose vignettes that match the general skill level of the participants, beginning with less complicated scenarios (e.g., the sudden death of a student from natural causes). As teams become more familiar with their roles and responsibilities and master the basic skills, they can undertake more challenging vignettes with more obstacles and unexpected elements. The goal is to challenge the teams without overwhelming them.

As crisis teams become better established, they should consider implementing crisis drills in the school setting. Even well-established teams benefit from regular practice through periodic drills. The drills should include community partners, such as police and rescue personnel, so that everyone who will be responding to a real crisis learns to work together effectively. If students will be involved in the crisis drill, or even if they may witness the drill, careful consideration should be given to how best to prepare the students so that they do not become alarmed by the activity.

Crisis vignettes should address the multiple demands of true crisis events. Be sure to pose situations that require the team to consider safety and security concerns, effective communication and information sharing, and psychological and emotional needs of students and staff. The challenge in responding to a crisis is to address these domains simultaneously and effectively.

In using the vignettes, either as table-top exercises or crisis drills, participants should review what they learned from the activity—strengths or assets that were identified, potential liabilities, or skill deficits that became apparent. It is also important to reflect on what the team learned about their group process: How were decisions made? Was the chair so directive that members did not have ample opportunity to voice their opinions? Was there so much emphasis on equal participation that decision making was compromised? How was conflict among team members perceived and managed? Reflecting on the process of working together is an important component of team building and promotes the development of properly functioning teams that can provide maximal support to each other and to members of the school community in an actual crisis.

Vignette A

A rainstorm has quickly and unexpectedly escalated into a violent thunderstorm. Before school staff can initiate any emergency dismissal procedures, a tornado-like wind slams into the school. The wind breaks numerous windows, causing injuries to staff and students from flying shards of glass. It rips away one section of wall, exposing two classrooms filled with students. Fallen trees sever electrical power to the school, and live wires are down outside the main entrance. The current situation: no lights, inoperable PA system, telephones in working order. There are telephones in the main office, teachers' room, nurse's office, and cafeteria. The nurse and office secretary are not in the building today.

Vignette B

On a school-sponsored outing to a large state park, a student wanders away from the group and drowns in a lake. The drowning victim was a popular student. Many classmates witness the rescue and the futile revival efforts while waiting for the bus to return. Rescue workers arriving on the scene hospitalize one teacher for shock.

Vignette C

A series of fights have broken out in the cafeteria during the second lunch and two students have injuries from what might have been a knife. Both are bleeding profusely. One staff member reports seeing a gun. Many of the students involved in the fights have left the school grounds without permission. The word among students is that the fights were gang-related and that more trouble will soon follow. Many students are milling outside the cafeteria and hallways. Several witnesses are visibly upset. The principal is away at an all-day conference on gang violence, and the school psychologist is at another school. Staff in the building include the nurse, school social worker, assistant principal, secretary, cafeteria staff, and teachers.

Vignette D

Late Wednesday evening, a staff member notifies the principal that Mark, a student at the school, is the victim of a shooting and has died only hours before. Mark's aunt, a staff member at the school, informed another staff member who, in turn, called the principal. The principal immediately notifies the co-chair of the school crisis team. Initial information is sketchy, but conversation with a representative of the local police force affirms that Mark's murder appears to be drug- or gang-related. Mark was an extremely popular student and had transferred from another school in the district earlier in the year. Staff had spoken to Mark just yesterday, at which time he mentioned that he was excited about the school dance scheduled for Friday evening. The funeral arrangements may not occur until Monday or Tuesday because of the legal issues involved and the long distances that relatives will be traveling.

Study Guide

The facilitator allows the group to read and discuss the vignette (in this case, Vignette D) for a few minutes. He then guides the group through the vignette by posing the following questions to elicit the bulleted points listed, probing or prompting as needed. After group discussion, he provides further elaboration of the vignette (noted as "Facilitator comments").

1. What needs to be done immediately (i.e., this evening)?

a. Who needs to be notified, when, and for what purpose?

- Notify crisis team members to plan emergency team meeting.

- Notify school faculty and staff about emergency staff meeting.

- Notify district crisis team, especially since the crisis involves more than one school.

- Contact police liaison concerning possible threat to students' safety.

b. Who should contact Mark's family and for what purpose?

- A school representative should express condolences, offer support, and provide referrals for counseling services for family members.

Facilitator comments: The co-chair of the crisis team contacts the Staff Notification Coordinator, who initiates the telephone tree and notifies all school faculty and staff of an emergency staff meeting Thursday morning (before the start of the school day). The chair of the team plans an emergency crisis team meeting to immediately precede the emergency staff meeting. She then notifies the district crisis team urging that a district representative contact Mark's former school. The District Chair apprises the District Coordinator of Counseling Services of the anticipated need for additional counseling and support staff for Thursday morning. The School Crisis Team Chair contacts the police liaison the following morning for further information and advice regarding physical safety of the students.

2. What needs to be done at the emergency crisis team meeting on Thursday?

- Review known information, including what police can provide.

- Review plan for responding to children's needs and reactions.

- Address issue of threats to students' safety, given possible gang involvement.

- Assess likely needs for counseling services for students and who will provide them. Consider role and staffing of support rooms.

- Determine if additional arrangements are needed for counseling or support staff.

- Discuss notification plans. Will the team hold a meeting for parents?

- Prepare notification letters for students and parents.

- Prepare a statement for the Communications Coordinator to read to phone callers.

- Discuss handling of press inquiries and prepare a press release, in collaboration with the District Media Coordinator.

- Plan the agenda for an emergency staff meeting. Remember to consider reactions of school staff.

- Schedule and plan for the next meeting of the school crisis team. Anticipate scheduling of a follow-up meeting for staff.

Facilitator comments: The crisis team, recognizing Mark's popularity at both his current and former school, anticipate a major schoolwide response. A team member contacts the District Coordinator of Counseling Services so that he can arrange for counseling staff of neighboring schools to be assigned to this school for the day, in order to staff the support rooms for the students. Support rooms are open with counselors in place by the start of the school day, which the principal announces to students over the public address system during homeroom. The crisis team schedules a follow-up meeting for the end of the school day. The principal has already scheduled an emergency staff meeting to immediately follow the crisis team meeting that morning, prior to the start of the school day.

3. What needs to be done at the emergency staff meeting on Thursday morning?

- Review information known and status report. Emphasize the need to control rumors.

- Solicit staff's reactions and provide appropriate support.

- Review the crisis team's plans for responding to students' needs and reactions.

- Address issues of students' safety.

- Review crowd management plans, especially if the team sees a threat to student safety.

- Review plans for providing counseling services and for defining guidelines and procedures for referral.

- Review and distribute notification announcements to students and parents.

- Discuss funeral attendance by students.

- Schedule a follow-up staff meeting.

Facilitator comments: During the staff meeting, one teacher asks if the staff should cancel the school dance, which is scheduled for the following evening. The staff decide to hold the dance as scheduled, but with additional staff assigned to the event. They plan a follow-up staff meeting for Monday afternoon.

4. **If you were the crisis team at Mark's *former* school, how would your plans differ?**

REFERENCES AND RESOURCES

American Academy of Pediatrics: Committee on Injury and Poison Prevention. (1992). Firearm injuries affecting the pediatric population. *Pediatrics, 89*(4), 788–790.

American Psychological Association. (1993). *Violence and youth: Psychology's response.* (Vol. 1). Washington, DC: Author.

Centers for Disease Control. (1992). *Youth suicide prevention and resource guide.* Atlanta, GA: Author.

Ewalt, P., & Perkins, L. (1979). The real experience of death among adolescents: An empirical study. *Social Casework: The Journal of Contemporary Social Work, 60,* 547–551.

Halprin, H. A. (1973). Crisis theory: A definitional study. *Community Mental Health Journal, 9,* 342–349.

Kline, M., Schonfeld, D. J., & Lichtenstein, R. (1995). Benefits and challenges of school-based crisis response teams. *Journal of School Health, 65,* 245–249.

Klingman, A. (1988). School community in disaster: Planning for intervention. *Journal of Community Psychology, 24*, 48–54.

Lichtenstein, R., Schonfeld, D. J., & Kline, M. (1994). School crisis response: Expecting the unexpected. *Educational Leadership, 52*(3) 79–83.

Lyons, J. A. (1987). Post-traumatic stress disorder in children and adolescents: A review of the literature. *Journal of Developmental and Behavioral Pediatrics, 8*, 349–356.

Mitchell, J. T. (1983). When disaster strikes: The critical incident stress debriefing process. *Journal of Emergency Medical Services 8*(1) 36–39.

Moriarty, A., Maeyama, R. G., & Fitzgerald, P. J. (1993). A CLEAR plan for school crisis management. *NASSP Bulletin, 77*(522) 17–22.

Newgass, S., & Schonfeld, D. J. (2000). School crisis intervention, crisis prevention, and crisis response. In A. Roberts (Ed.), *Crisis intervention handbook: Assessment, treatment, and research* (2nd edition) (pp. 209–228). New York: Oxford University Press.

New Haven Public Schools. (1992). *Social development project, 1991–1992 evaluation report.* New Haven, CT: Author.

Pastore, D., Fisher, M., & Friedman, S. (1991). Violence and mental health risks among urban high school students. *Journal of Developmental and Behavioral Pediatrics, 12*(4) 273–274.

Petersen, S., & Straub, R. L. (1992). *School crisis survival guide: Management techniques and materials for counselors and administrators.* West Nyack, NY: Center for Applied Research in Education.

Pitcher, G., & Poland, S. (1992). *Crisis intervention in the schools.* New York: Guilford Press.

Poland, S. (1994). The role of school crisis intervention teams to prevent and reduce school violence and trauma. *School Psychology
Review, 23*, 175–189.

Portis, M., & Portis, R. (1992). Ready for anything. *American School
Board Journal, 179*(11) 41–43.

Rapoport, L. (1965). The state of crisis: Some theoretical considerations. In M. J. Parad (Ed.), *Crisis intervention: Selected readings.*
New York: Family Service Association of America.

Schonfeld, D. J. (2002). Supporting adolescents in times of national
crisis: Potential roles for adolescent healthcare providers.
Journal of Adolescent Health, 30(5), 302–307.

Schonfeld, D. J. (1989). Crisis intervention for bereavement support:
A model of intervention in the children's school. *Clinical
Pediatrics 28*, 27–33.

Schonfeld, D. J. (1993). Talking with children about death. *Journal of
Pediatric Health Care, 7*, 269–274.

Schonfeld, D. J., & Kappelman, M. (1992). Teaching elementary
schoolers about death: The toughest lesson. *Education Digest
58*(4) 16–20.

Schonfeld, D. J., Kline, M., & Members of the Crisis Intervention
Committee. (1994). School-based crisis intervention: An orga-
nizational model. *Crisis Intervention and Time-Limited
Treatment, 1*, 155–166.

Sheley, J., McGee, Z., & Wright, J. (1992). Gun-related violence in and
around inner city schools. *American Journal of Diseases of
Children, 146*, 677–682.

Taylor, L., Harik, V., & Zuckerman, B. (1992). Exposure to violence
among inner city parents and young children. *American
Journal of Diseases of Children, 146*, 487.

About the Authors

DAVID J. SCHONFELD is associate professor, Departments of Pediatrics and Child Study Center, Yale University School of Medicine, 333 Cedar St., P.O. Box 208064, New Haven, CT 06520-8064. Schonfeld is also program coordinator of the School Crisis Prevention and Response Initiative of the National Center for Children Exposed to Violence. E-mail: david.schonfeld@yale.edu.

ROBERT LICHTENSTEIN is consultant for School Psychology and School Social Work, Connecticut State Department of Education, 25 Industrial Park Road, Middletown, CT 06457. E-mail: Bob.Lichtenstein@po.state.ct.us.

MARSHA KLINE PRUETT is a research scientist in the Law and Psychiatry Division of Yale University School of Medicine,

Connecticut Mental Health Center, 34 Park St., New Haven, CT 06508. E-mail: Marsha.Pruett@po.state.ct.us.

DEE SPEESE-LINEHAN is supervisor of the Social Development Department of New Haven Public Schools, 250 Greene St., New Haven, CT 06511. E-mail: dee.speeselinehan@newhaven. kiz.ct.us.

Related ASCD Resources: Crisis Planning

At the time of publication, the following ASCD resources were available; for the most up-to-date information about ASCD resources, go to www.ascd.org. ASCD stock numbers are noted in parentheses.

Audiotapes

Beyond the Crisis Management Plan by Edward Seifert (#200107)

Networks

Visit the ASCD Web site (www.ascd.org) and click on About ASCD. Under the header of Your Partnership with ASCD, click on Networks for information about professional educators who have formed groups around topics, including "Character Education" and "Global Education." Look in the "Network Directory" for current facilitators' addresses and phone numbers.

Print Products

Communicating with the Public: A Guide for School Leaders by Anne Meek (#199052)

Quick Reference: Seven Important Steps to Take in a Crisis by Educational Service District 105, Yakima, Washington (#197176)

Quick Response: A Step-by-Step Guide to Crisis Management for Principals, Counselors, and Teachers by Educational Service District 105, Yakima, Washington (#197175)

Videotapes

A Safe Place to Learn: Crisis Response and School Safety Planning by Bob Watson (#496062)

For more information, visit us on the World Wide Web (http://www.ascd.org), send an e-mail message to member@ascd.org, call the ASCD Service Center (1-800-933-ASCD or 703-578-9600, then press 2), send a fax to 703-575-5400, or write to Information Services, ASCD, 1703 N. Beauregard St., Alexandria, VA 22311-1714 USA.